Outside, You Notice

by Erin Alladin
Illustrated by Andrea Blinick

pajamapress

First published in Canada and the United States in 2021

Text copyright © 2021 Erin Alladin
Illustration copyright © 2021 Andrea Blinick
This edition copyright © 2021 Pajama Press Inc.
This is a first edition.

10 9 8 7 6 5 4 3 2 1

www.pajamapress.ca   info@pajamapress.ca

Canada Council   Conseil des arts
for the Arts   du Canada

OA ONTARIO ARTS COUNCIL
CONSEIL DES ARTS DE L'ONTARIO
an Ontario government agency
un organisme du gouvernement de l'Ontario

Canadä

The publisher gratefully acknowledges the support of the Canada Council for the Arts and the Ontario Arts Council for its publishing program. We acknowledge the financial support of the Government of Canada through the Canada Book Fund (CBF) for our publishing activities.

Library and Archives Canada Cataloguing in Publication
Title: Outside, you notice / by Erin Alladin ; illustrated by Andrea Blinick.
Names: Alladin, Erin, 1989- author. | Blinick, Andrea, 1979- illustrator.
Description: First edition.
Identifiers: Canadiana 20200343548 | ISBN 9781772781939 (hardcover)
Subjects: LCSH: Nature—Miscellanea—Juvenile literature. | LCSH: Natural history—Miscellanea—Juvenile literature. | LCSH: Nature—Juvenile literature. | LCSH: Natural history—Juvenile literature.
Classification: LCC QH48 .A45 2021 | DDC j508—dc23

Publisher Cataloging-in-Publication Data (U.S.)
Names: Alladin, Erin, 1989-, author. | Blinick, Andrea, 1979-, illustrator.
Title: Outside, You Notice / by Erin Alladin; illustrated by Andrea Blinick.
Description: Toronto, Ontario Canada : Pajama Press, 2021. | Summary: "Poetic nonfiction text describes a child's sensory experience of various kinds of outdoor space. On each spread, facts related to observation center on a particular theme, including rain, animal homes, fruit, soil, flowers, seeds, water, roots, leaves, vegetables, pollinators, and the benefits of spending time outdoors" -- Provided by publisher.
Identifiers: ISBN 978-1-77278-193-9 (hardcover)
Subjects: LCSH: Senses and sensation – Juvenile literature. | Outdoor life – Juvenile literature. | BISAC: JUVENILE NONFICTION / Science & Nature / General. | JUVENILE NONFICTION / Gardening. | JUVENILE NONFICTION / Animals / General.
Classification: LCC QP434.A453 | DDC 612.8 – dc23

Cover and book design—Rebecca Bender

Manufactured by Qualibre Inc./Printplus
Printed in China

Original art created
with gouache, colored pencil,
collage, and chalk pastel

Pajama Press Inc.
469 Richmond St. E, Toronto, ON M5A 1R1

Distributed in Canada by UTP Distribution
5201 Dufferin Street Toronto, Ontario Canada, M3H 5T8

Distributed in the U.S. by Ingram Publisher Services
1 Ingram Blvd. La Vergne, TN 37086, USA

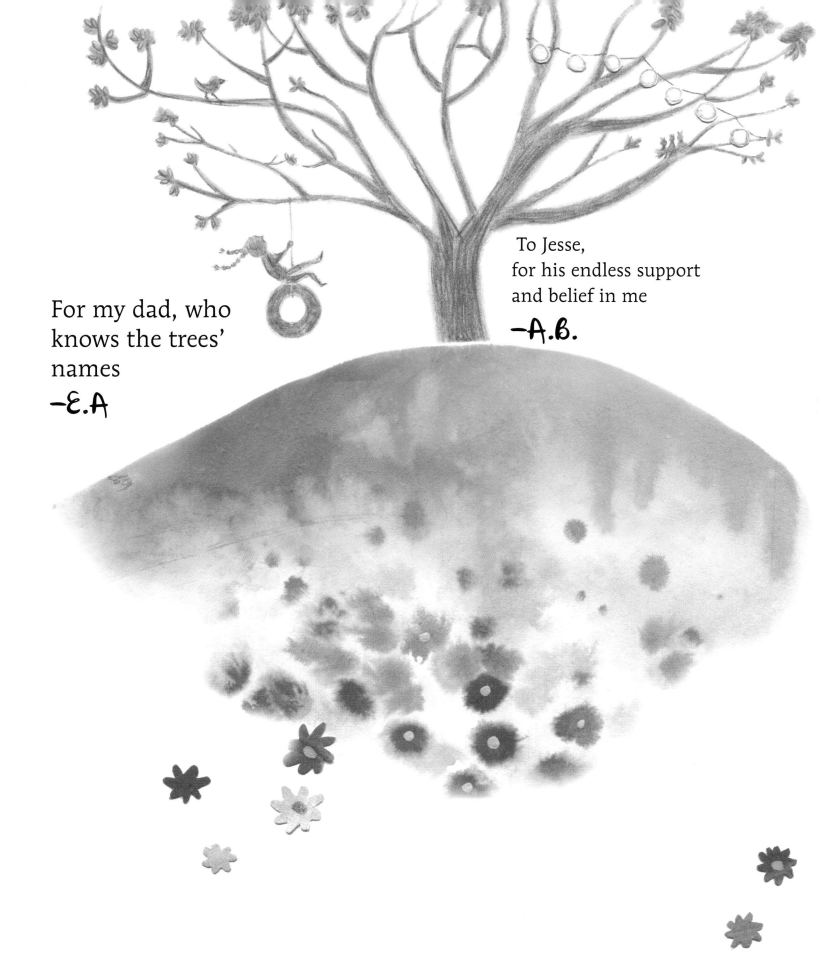

For my dad, who knows the trees' names

−E.A

To Jesse,
for his endless support
and belief in me

−A.B.

Outside,
You notice things—

How after the rain
Everything smells greener

Do you know what rain smells like? The smell is partly made of oils released by plants.

Some plants have leaves shaped like funnels to help catch rainwater.

Some trees have so many leaves that the ground around the trunk stays dry even during heavy rain.

Plants drink water through their roots.

How lots of little noises—
Birds singing
Bees buzzing
Squirrels running—
Make up one big quiet

Rabbits dig underground homes, called warrens, with lots of exit holes.

Piles of brush are important homes for many animals, including chipmunks, snakes, and birds.

Some kinds of bees live in hives with hundreds of other bees. Other kinds live alone in hollow stems.

Squirrels make ball-shaped nests high in the forks of tree branches.

Many animals make homes in old woodpecker holes.

How a strawberry
Tastes sweetest
When you pick it yourself
And eat it still warm
From the sun

A fruit is the part of a plant that produces seeds. Even peppers and tomatoes are fruits!

Fruit trees that are pruned to stay small still make full-sized fruit.

Plants make tasty fruits so that birds and animals will eat them and carry the seeds to new places.

Every fruit starts out as a flower.

Fruit tastes sweetest when it has ripened during sunny weather.

How digging the earth
Until it's up to your elbows
And even behind your ears
Makes you feel more proud
Than dirty
(Though you still need a bath)

When dead plants fall on the ground, tiny creatures eat them and turn them into soil. We call this decomposing.

Scientists have found that getting soil on our skin can make humans feel happier.

Soil is a mixture of tiny
pieces of rock and tiny
pieces of decomposed plants.

Dark-colored soil has more
decomposed plants in it than
light-colored soil.

If you dig a deep hole, you will
find many layers of soil that
get more and more rocky.

You notice that a dandelion
Is just as golden
As a marigold

The color, smell, and shape of flowers are all designed to attract bees and other pollinators.

Many plants will bloom more if their flowers are picked often.

Some flowers only
bloom at night,
when they are
pollinated by moths
or bats.

The petals of some flowers,
like violets, clover, mint, and
pansies, can be eaten.

Broccoli is actually
a flower.

Dandelions can be
eaten, and they are
extremely healthy.

That seeds cupped in your hand
Feel like the tiniest
    And most important
Things in the world

Even before it sprouts, a plant's first leaves are rolled up tight inside its seed.

If they are stored in a cool and dry place, seeds can survive for thousands of years.

Seeds have many tricks to find their own space to grow. Dandelions use fluff that carries them on the wind. Touch-me-not seed pods explode when they are ripe. Burs stick to clothing and animal fur.

When a seed is soaked in water, it swells up. When it's full of water, the seed knows it's time to grow.

You notice that the sound of water
Tumbling over itself
Soothes and stills
Your own tumbling mind

Water always flows downhill. Most of it eventually ends up in the ocean.

Streams and rivers create areas that are fertile (that can grow plants well) because they carry nutrients from one place to another.

Every living thing on earth needs water to survive.

Rivers flow through the ground as well as on top of it.

You notice
    If you're nosy
That there's a lot
more going on
Under your feet
Than around them

Plants get some of the food they need from fungus that lives around their roots. The plants attract the fungus by feeding it sugar.

Many roots, like carrots, get bigger all summer because the plant is using them to store food.

Earthworms have no teeth. They depend on microbes to break food down before they can eat it. They eat the microbes too.

A single tablespoon of healthy soil contains billions of tiny creatures.

You notice that maple leaves
are strong
And cast sharp shadows
But aspen leaves tremble
So that bits of sunlight
Dance in their shade

Plants are the only living things
on earth that can make their own
food. Their leaves use sunlight,
air, and water to make sugar.

Pine needles are a special kind of leaf.

Most leaves are flat because this lets them absorb lots of sunlight.

The veins in leaves transport water and food.

That you never really knew the
color orange—
Not really—
Until you saw a carrot
Still spotted with black earth

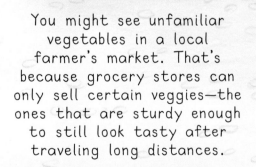

You might see unfamiliar
vegetables in a local
farmer's market. That's
because grocery stores can
only sell certain veggies—the
ones that are sturdy enough
to still look tasty after
traveling long distances.

Honeybees are the most famous pollinators, but many flowers need to be visited by bumblebees, flies, hummingbirds, butterflies, moths, or bats instead.

Many grasses are pollinated by the wind blowing through their flowers.

Tube-shaped flowers can only be pollinated by creatures with long tongues, like hummingbirds.

Outside, you notice
The breath in your body
Your feet on the ground
Your self in the world

Being exposed to lots of microbes in the outdoors can help your immune system get better at fighting sickness.

Scientists have proven that spending time in nature is good for the health of your body and your mind.

People who spend time in nature feel less anxiety and stress.

When you're outside, you are often looking at things that are far away. This lets your eyes relax and use different muscles than usual.

Being outside helps you get healthy exercise.

Listening to nature sounds can help you feel calm and relaxed. So can looking at plants, sky, or water.

And then you can bloom

There are lots of ways to get outside! Here are some of the places shown in this book: